Despite the intense nature of this story I support and respect the men and women of law enforcement as long as they have committed no crimes.

-Terry Dante

ONE OF US

As I began my long walk toward the office of Police Chief Lawrence many thoughts raced through my mind. Did I do the right thing? Was I really going to avoid time behind bars? Would I still be a police officer after this meeting was over? But most of all, was everything Lawrence said about laws and policies changing within departments across the nation true?

My killings were multiple and performed with deadly force but justified in the eyes of the public. My name is Ace McMillan, and I am in this situation because I successfully brought down the corrupt officers in my police force as well as many others. A lot of those fellow officers are dead, the surviving few are going to serve life sentences in prison with no special arrangements.

Before I go any deeper into the mass killings I had committed, let me start from the

beginning of my career, the experiences that motivated me to fight back, and my overall

agenda. I had graduated with a bachelor's degree in criminal justice, eventually I went on to

finish the police academy. Employers were so impressed with my resume that I was

immediately hired on and assigned to the mean streets of Tampa, Florida.

So here I am two months with the force, Friday night 10pm. Despite my credentials I

had to start from the bottom. Odd work schedule, busting bad drivers, I was also on my ninety

day probation period. Typical shift for a rookie cop however, I could not have been paired up

with a supervisor as hip as the one my captain had assigned. His name was Lieutenant Reggae Kenneth. Reggae was a Vietnam vet in his early sixties, he would always tell me old war stories

whenever we were having a slow work night. Despite the horrific nature of his experiences in

Vietnam he almost always had a smile on his face when he told those stories. Reggaes

personality was so cheerful and laid back I would have thought he was a blues musician. After

all his mannerisms were quite reminiscent of the late great "Screamin Jay Hawkins."

As nice as these slow work nights had been, they would soon come to an end. About

Seventy-five days into my probation period Reggae and I got a call about a "stolen" car.

Despite my intensity and free hand constantly patting the gun in my holster Reggae sat in his

seat as if it were just another day at the office. "McMillan good buddy, put both of your hands

on the steering wheel!" He said in his usual gentle tone. Although he was sporting his

traditional grin while giving orders I cooperated without arguing. "Yes sir Lieutenant," I replied.

"You know something McMillan, you need to relax. I mean come on, were gonna catch these

guys, if you don't learn to loosen up, you ain't gonna live to see forty. And don't call me sir or

Lieutenant, just call me Reggae."

Sure enough Reggae was right we did catch the two offenders. The driver would soon crash the stolen vehicle into a brick wall in an ally way. I kept the sirens on while Reggae and I exited the cruiser. I drew my gun and demanded the driver to exit the vehicle. "COME OUT WITH YOUR HANDS UP!" I yelled. The young driver exited the vehicle without a fight and laid his hands on the roof of the car. I slowly approached him while Reggae calmly walked toward the other side of the car aiming his gun at the vehicles passenger. I proceeded to cuff the drivers hands behind his back. I patted him down and found no weapons in his possession. I escorted him to the back of my cruiser and read him his rights before closing the door.

Meanwhile Reggae gave the same command to the passenger. The passenger was cooperative until he had his back facing Reggae. He quickly spun around and kicked Reggae in his shin as Reggae slowly fell toward the ground the offender reached for the gun in Reggaes

holster. Before he could successfully grab hold of the piece I was above him with my gun

pointing directly at his head. “HANDS IN THE AIR PAL!” Nervously, the passenger of the vehicle

put his hands in the air and looked directly at me shaking in fear. “What’s your name?” I asked

him in a stern tone. “Buh-Billy” He replied fearfully.

Instead of escorting him to my cruiser I aimed my gun at his right knee cap and fired.

As he fell to the ground screaming in agony I stood over him and proceeded to aim my gun at

his forehead. I wasn’t going to read him his rights, I was going to sentence this thug to death.

As I was getting ready to squeeze the trigger Reggae intervened and grabbed the guns barrel.

Despite the heat of the moment he was still as calm and collected as he has always been.

“Ace, put the gun away and call for an ambulance.” I did what I was told and I called for an

Ambulance. In no time at all the ambulance had showed up and taken Billy away. After that

Reggae and I got in the cruiser and headed toward Olson Road Jail to get the driver processed

into the jails system. At around 1:30 in the morning Reggae and I had left the jail and headed

home, or so I thought.

"Ace I want to have a little talk with you about tonight's performance!" This was an

unusual tone for Reggae to take with me, he no longer had a cool laid back attitude like

"Screamin Jay Hawkins" now he reminded me of "Louis Gossett Jr." from "Iron eagle." "Pull into

this diner on your right Ace."

I parked in the diners lot, as I pulled into a parking space Reggae proceeded to chew me

out. "GOD DAMMIT MCMILLAN, WHAT THE HELL WERE YOU TRYING TO PULL BACK THERE?

YOU'RE A COP NOT JUDGE JURY AND EXECUTIONER! JESUS CHRIST I THOUGHT YOU WERE

BETTER THAN THIS, BUT NO YOU'RE JUST SOME YOUNG GUY WITH A CHIP ON HIS SHOULDER

WHOSE SEEN TOO MANY MOVIES!" I got the feeling he was done with his rant so I decided now was a good time to say my piece.

“Well Reggae I was just angry because he had every intention to kill you and I’m sure he would have tried to kill me afterward.” Instead of yelling Reggae smiled and nodded then thanked me for saving his life. Reggae reached over and patted me on the shoulder and said “Ok Ace I’ll give you that however you could have easily apprehended him. When you had your gun pointed at him I saw the fear in his eyes, he would have surrendered without a fight. I’ll do everything I can to make sure you stay on the force but I’m sure the captain will want to have a few words with you.

Listen Ace, I don’t know about you but I’m hungry what do you say you and me step into this diner for an early morning breakfast? This one is on me as long as you tell me a little more about yourself.” “What would you like to know?” I asked. “I’ll let you know when I’ve heard enough!” He replied. As we entered the diner we were immediately given a table, after all, it was about 2 a.m. in the morning and the only people in a diner at this hour besides off

duty cops were young adults, and drunks just coming from bars looking for a place to eat.

As we sat down and looked through our menus Reggae wasted no time twisting my arm

for information about my life story. "Alright Ace talk to me. You have this attitude like you are

running from something. I can see it in your eyes."

"Well Reggae if you must know there are some things in my past I haven't exactly let go of."

"Ok tell me all about it." Said Reggae. I told Reggae my story, I was involved in an incident that

would forever change my life. I was twenty-two years old and I met a strange woman on the

internet for sex at a motel somewhere in Polk County. After the sex was over I made it clear

that I didn't want to be her boyfriend. She got angry and I left the motel. I went to the leasing

office to see if I had to speak with the woman at the front desk. The name "Sara" was written on her nametag. She was having quite a disturbing conversation on the phone. "Do you want me to call the authorities?" She said. I knew for a fact this had something to do with me, sure enough I was right.

"The woman you were in the room with said that you hurt her." Said Sara. "I did no such thing, she's lying!" I replied. "Well I wasn't there so I can't speak for any of you." "Upon those comments I left the office and headed toward my car. As I rushed through the parking lot I saw the woman(let's call her Lana)who made false complaints about me head down the stairs."

"Hey sweetie how are you?" Cried Lana. "Lana, did you make complaints about me to the woman at the front desk?" "No!" Lana replied. "Good, go in the leasing office with me and tell her everything is cool." I demanded. "No get away from me!" With that Lana went back to the room and locked the door.

With that I went into the leasing office and told Sara that I had done nothing wrong, and that Lana came out of the motel room and briefly spoke to me. "Oh I saw her!" Said Sara.

"Yeah for somebody who claims that you harmed her she didn't seem too upset. She must be

crazy!" I felt overcome by a sense of relief but for some reason I started crying. At that

moment Sara took pity on me. "Oh honey it's alright nothing's going to happen just try to

relax." I sat down and trembled with anxiety.

Sara said and did everything she could to get me to relax, she even complimented me

on my looks. "You know I don't understand why a guy like you needs to go on the internet to

find a date." She said. I smiled a little bit but I was incredibly scared. I know I hadn't done

anything wrong but I knew things were going to be humiliating. After all, Gina's mom was a cop.

I sat there and waited for what seemed like eternity. Sara's husband Ron popped up and asked

what was going on. He saw I was crying real hard and I explained the situation and he stood

over me and said "Hey man it's going to be ok, just take it easy." Ron then informed me that unfortunately they did have to call the cops.

I continued to wait, after about an hour a few Polk County Sheriffs deputies showed up.

Around that time Gina was in the parking lot. The expression on her face when she saw me and

the discomfort she must've felt when the police approached her. "Maam I need to ask you a

few questions." Said the first deputy. His name was Officer Parsons. "Fuck this I'm out of here!"

Replied Lana. "Uh miss you need to stick around, we were called here for a reason." Said Officer

Parsons. Lana pointed at me and said "That man in there dragged me up those stairs busted the

door down threw me on the bed and forced himself on me." Sara however interrupted and said

"That's not what happened! Her and the gentleman sitting down came in there and paid for a

key to the room I assigned them." Sara and her husband came inside and swore to me things

would be ok. But I knew for a fact that I wasn't out of the woods.

Officer Parsons approached me and told me to step outside. "Mr. McMillan you are not

under arrest but we will have to detain you until the detective shows up." With that I was

cuffed and placed in the back of his cruiser and I sat there for what seemed like forever.

Eventually the detective showed up and I was taken out of the cruiser. Officer Parsons talked

with me for a bit and didn't understand why I wasted my time coming to a shit hole of a town

as he put it. All I did was laugh nervously and shrug my shoulders. Then he shook his head and

said "Seriously man you could have picked better things to do with your day." In the midst of

our conversation I kept glancing toward the detective's activity on the other side of the parking

lot. He was speaking with Lana unfortunately I could not here the conversation that was

ensuing.

At that moment Officer Parsons looked at me and read me my rights. I stood up straight

and didn't say a word. Soon the detective would make his way over to my direction and listen to my side of the story. “Mr. McMillan?” He asked. “Yes Sir?” I said nervously. “My name is Detective Harrington how are you this evening?” “I’ve had better Detective.” “I can understand Sir. I’m going to need you to make a recorded statement. What exactly happened in your motel Room?” “Well I met Lana on an internet dating site and we agreed to meet here to have sex. She didn’t take it too well when I told her I didn’t want to be her boyfriend.” “So in other words you came here for a one night stand?” “Yes Sir that’s exactly why I came here.” “Ok Mr. McMillan here is the situation it took a while but Lana admitted to lying about what happened between you two. She told me she lied because she wanted to avoid slack for cheating on her boyfriend.”

“Boyfriend?” I asked. “Yes that’s correct. Mr. McMillan sit tight for a minute I have to have a few words with my supervisor, but just so you know you are not under arrest.” Within no time Detective Harrington came back outside and told me to drive home safely and try to

relax. I got in my car and headed back to Tampa. As I headed west on I-4 I looked long and hard

at the night sky and the hills. I knew from that point on I would never be the same. I made it

home before midnight. I was going to call in sick to work the next day but I sucked it up and

went in to work as if nothing happened. I will admit what I did was stupid but that was no

excuse for that woman to try and ruin my life. "Ace, I am really sorry to hear about your

experience, what happened from there?" Asked Reggae. "Well I have never told my family

about this experience but not a day goes by when I don't think about it. I thought about going

after Lana to get revenge for quite some time. But then another part of me thought about

suicide in hopes that it would raise awareness for people who have been victims of rape and

abuse accusations."

"Don't say that, don't even think that!" Reggae said after banging his fist on the table

Reggae looked at me with sadness in his eyes as if to tell me things were going to be ok.

However when he spoke he told me something I didn't expect to hear. "Ace, when I look at you I sometimes get the feeling that you are going to be another Rick Thompson." "Who is Rick Thompson?" I asked. "Rick Thompson is a cop who overcame odds and became a hero to police officers and citizens in his hometown. Some call him "The Grim Reaper With A Badge." As Reggae went on about Rick Thompson I listened with amazement and admiration. When Reggae finished the story he looked at me and said "Don't get any ideas! You are in enough trouble as it is." With that we left the diner and I dropped Reggae off at his house then I headed home.

The next day I was called into the Captain Hamilton's office. Hamilton was a short fat guy with a mustache who looked like he was going to lose his hair any second. "Well McMillan the good news is Billy's parents don't want to sue you or the department. However Ace I am

going to have to put you on paid leave." I breathed a huge sigh of relief however the meeting

was far from over. "McMillan you need to get your act together. Keep your temper in check, I

can't have my officers taking the law into their hands." "Yes sir." I replied. With that I left

Hamilton's office and drove to the gym. Even after all these years weightlifting was still my

number one hobby. After I finished my workout I headed home and zoned out in my bedroom.

I took a long hard look at myself. Although I have great friends and family I knew that at

the end of the day I was just a man fueled by hatred of demons from my past. I laid back on my

bed and started daydreaming. I thought about the moment in my childhood when I had

developed a bizarre curiosity with killing. Not good people of course, just the bad. I particularly

remember my mom and dad snapping at me because I said how I wanted to kill someone. I can't remember who I was talking about or why I said it but my parents wanted to make sure I

would never speak in such a manner ever again. As I got older I would continue to stay out of

trouble but I still maintained my "I want to kill people attitude." Watching the news and

reading the paper wasn't much comfort either. Especially when there are stories about

murderers, rapists, and white collar criminals receiving either psychiatric treatment or

promotions instead of harsh prison sentences. Also police officers who commit crimes and

receive no jail time, much less job termination. These were the stories gave me a sense of

bloodlust

Not to mention my traumatic experience of a crazed woman accusing me of rape. That's

when I decided to put two and two together. I would go back to school, earn my degree in

criminal justice and become a police officer. It made perfect since, cops practically get away

with murder so why not take advantage of it? Not only would I prey on civilian offenders but I would go after other cops as well. Sooner or later I was going to bring crime to its knees.

In the meantime however I had a month's worth of paid vacation to enjoy.

My vacation ultimately came to an end and I was back on the beat with Reggae. "Ace it's

great to have you back. Just so you know I spoke very highly about you to the captain, I hope he

wasn't too rough on you." "Oh no everything is fine Reggae." With that Reggae and I were

placed in separate cruisers heading east bound on Fowler. We parked our cars in a shopping

center just past 22nd avenue. An hour or so went by sure enough one person did go over the

speed limit. Reggae called it in the air and pulled the driver over. "Watch and learn rookie!" He

said to me over his radio. I smiled and laughed. Unfortunately something big was about to go

down. Reggae and I received calls on our radio about a robbery in progress at the Wachovia

bank past 56th street. Reggae and I turned on our sirens and headed further east on Fowler.

In no time at all we pulled into the bank. "Ace listen to me carefully park your car in the back and slowly sneak around to the front of the bank. I will park around the front and speak to to the robber through the megaphone." I did as I was told and went to the back. This actually wasn't a bad idea I would say that Reggae is a much better negotiator than I am, plus my adrenaline was pumping hard. I slowly lurked around the building ready to kill. As I made my way closer to the front I saw the door slowly open. The bank robber emerged from the bank however he wasn't alone, he had a hostage. "Drop your weapon and let the woman go." Demanded Reggae. "I have a better idea, put down your gun and then I'll let the woman go free." Replied the gunman. I assessed the situation very carefully, even though he had a hostage she was covering his left side, unfortunately for him I was on his right side. On top of that he wasn't aware of my presence. I waited for him to come closer to the right so I could bring him down and save the female hostage. Sure enough the opportunity arose, I put my gun

to the back of his head and pulled the trigger.

Bits of his brain matter and blood exploded through the hole in his head after the

bullet tore through his skull. His body slowly hit the ground while the terrified woman ran in

terror. I looked closely at the dead body that lay before me. I had just ended a human life, he

deserved to die but I felt a lot of pain and discomfort at that moment. After I collected my

thoughts I grabbed my radio and called for an ambulance and told them to bring a body bag.

The ambulance showed up pretty quick even though I wanted to sit down and be alone with my

thoughts Reggae and I had a job to do which meant we had to go check on the bank employees

and customers to make sure everyone was ok. “Are you ok to drive back to the station?” Asked

Reggae. “I’ll be fine Reggae.” I shook it off and drove back to the station.

I made it back to the station at around 5 in the afternoon, Captain Hamilton was waiting to speak with me. “McMillan, great job you’re a better cop than I have given you credit for.

Even when someone deserves to die it’s not an easy job to do, take tomorrow off. You

need some time to yourself.” Yes sir,” I replied. I headed out of the building and went home

to try and sleep off what had happened earlier. Believe it or not every time I tried to fall asleep

all I saw was the face of the man I had killed.

I decided to go do some grocery shopping and then have a movie night by myself. Even

though I had committed no crimes I felt so different and disconnected from those around me.

Despite my circle of friends I was always kind of a loner, after my first kill I felt even more alone.

When I got home I threw some food in the oven and decided to watch “Death Wish” starring

The late Charles Bronson. I had seen this movie numerous times and I never grew tired of it. I

remember when I saw this movie at a young age loving his character, a man who was tired of street thugs preying on the innocent while the police made little to no effort to help those they

were sworn to protect. Pretty soon my feelings of despair and discomfort over the life I had

taken earlier that day had faded. My desires to kill had eventually come back.

Before I knew it my day off had ended and I was back at work. I met up with Reggae at

the shooting range. After firing a few rounds at our targets Reggae had a few words with me

about what happened two days ago. "Ace if you need to talk to me I am always here for you."

"Thank you Reggae but I'm going to be ok." We walked back into the station and headed

toward our desks. When I saw the stack of paperwork on my desk I was wishing more and

more I wouldn't have had to kill that bank robber. As I thumbed through my paperwork I

noticed something; it had all been filled out. I went to Reggae and asked if he knew anything

about the situation with my paperwork. "Well Ace during your day off I took care of that stuff for you." I patted him on the shoulder and said "Reggae lets you and me go out to dinner

later and have a drink or two on the side, I owe you." "Thanks Ace, in the meant time you can

clean up my office." Replied Reggae while laughing and pointing to a mop and bucket.

As I was mopping the floors of Reggaes office I laughed at him and said "Man how

Bad did you piss off the janitor for him to not clean your office? This place is a dump!" "You

know Ace since you are really digging this job why don't you wash my car afterward?" With that

Reggae laughed and gave me the finger. "All kidding aside Ace I will have a few drinks with you

putting up with your shit for nearly a year has driven me to drinking." "So you're a comedian in

your spare time?" I laughed. "Ace, put the mop down and let's get out of here so I can drink you

under the table." We clocked out and headed toward the nearest sports bar.

As we made our way toward the exit I heard a harsh arrogant voice call out to me. "Well look who it is, the young screw up and his over the hill supervisor." I turned around to go face my rude co-worker and give him my two cents but Reggae grabbed my shoulder and said "Ace don't pay any attention to Martinez, he just has a bad attitude." Even though I had seen Martinez day in day out for nearly a year this was the first time he had ever spoken a word to me. Various people told me he was a pretentious ass but I ignored them because I didn't want to contribute to gossip. But in this case the facts really added up. Antonio Jose Martinez had been on the force a little longer than me but I was more respected by others. After all I had him beat when it came to ethics, marksmanship, and hand to hand combat.

I was going to take Reggaes advice and simply walk away but Martinez didn't take to kindly to Reggaes comment. "What did you say old man?" Antonio approached both of us like he wanted to fight. "Antonio, we don't want any trouble. Besides you can't go around acting confrontational toward others just because they point out your attitude problem. Also I am a

lieutenant so don't you dare come walking up to me sticking your chest out like you want to

fight." Antonio however didn't back off he was about to wave his finger at Reggaes face and

talk more trash but I stepped between them and spoke up. "You know something Antonio,

Reggae is right you do have a bad attitude, why don't you get back to work and let Reggae and I

get on with our day." "YOU SON OF A BITCH!" No sooner did he yell in my face he grabbed my

shirt I responded by grabbing wrist while pressing my thumb into the area between his wrist

and the palm of his hand. I followed up by throwing a right jab directly into his nose.

He hit the floor instantly putting his hands over his bloody nose howling in pain. I put my

foot on his sternum and looked down at him and proceeded to talk down to him.

"Hey Martinez, maybe you should join Reggae and I at the bar, it'll take a lot of booze to get your mind off the ass kicking I just gave you." As I was finally getting ready to leave

the station I heard Hamilton angrily call Martinez and I into his office. "MCMILLAN, MARTINEZ

MARCH YOUR ASSES IN HERE!" Feeling a little cocky I took my sweet time heading toward the

captains office. When I made it to the doorway I turned around and saw that Martinez was still

laying down on the floor in pain. I looked at him for a while and said "You heard the captain

march your ass in here!" I took my seat and within a few minutes I was joined by Martinez

carrying tissues and a bag of ice for his nose.

"Alright you two what the hell happened out there?" "Well since Martinez over here is

still in a lot of pain I will say my piece first. Martinez ran his mouth and I showed him the error

of his ways, pretty cut and dry if you ask me." "Well Ace this is how I see it you have a real

attitude problem, you are going to attend anger management this coming Monday. As for you

Martinez you aren't much better, you can't go around picking fights with your co-workers you need to familiarize yourself with proper ethics. Ace before Martinez leaves take a good look

at what you've done to him, he has to be about a hundred and fifty pounds you clearly have a

hundred pound advantage on him. Not to mention your background in the martial arts,

according to your files you have a black belt in judo and you have practiced other forms of

martial arts. Your hands are registered lethal weapons, SAVE IT FOR EMERGENCIES!" "Yes sir

Hamilton." "Ok now get out of my office, not you Ace sit back down."

Right then and there I thought I was going to get hit with a huge suspension or

administrative leave. Then I thought "Oh no, Hamilton is going to load me down with stacks and

stacks of paperwork. Hamilton stood in front of his door with his back facing me. Then he

turned around and slowly walked back toward his desk. He looked at me for a second and said

something I didn't expect. "Sorry I went off on you like that McMillan, I had to make Martinez think that I actually have respect for him. Ace I want to take this time to thank you for what you

did." Although I was confused I smiled and nodded at Hamilton. "Just hear me out Ace, its

people like Martinez that give this force a bad name. I've tried to fire him numerous times but

he keeps getting his job back despite the severity of his actions. "What has he done Captain?"

"Ace what I am about to tell you doesn't leave my office. I'll put it to you like this you and

Reggae aren't the only people he has picked fights with. He does this sort of thing with citizens

even over the most minor of things. Whether it's yielding at a stop sign, telling minors to obey

their curfew, or just talking to people involved in a domestic dispute, he tries to bully and

intimidate just so he has a reason to arrest someone.

Sadly he isn't the only one on the force to pull this kind of shit. There are at least a few

people on the force like Martinez in fact they are all friends with Martinez. And as long as we

have Police Panels Martinez and others like him will never lose their jobs. Personally Ace I wish somebody would take out Martinez and anyone else who disrespects the badge."

"So I guess you don't support the brotherhood mentality either huh?" "No Ace I don't. Please

do me a favor and keep an eye on Martinez." "Sir, what about the others you had mentioned?"

"Well discuss them on Monday Ace, get out of here its Friday so make the most of today and

enjoy your weekend. Oh one more thing, Martinez and a few people are still outside so when

you exit my office I have to make everyone think that I am chewing you out so get ready for me

to start yelling again."

As I headed out Hamilton got right back into character. "REMEMBER ACE DON'T FUCK

WITH ME, I CAN TAKE YOUR BADGE ANYTIME I WANT!" As I left the building there was silence

in the air. Everyone, including a bloodied up Martinez were staring at me. I saw a look of shock

on some faces, contempt in the eyes of Martinez, admiration amongst those who liked me,

Reggae on the other hand looked quite disappointed in me. "Ace, I'll drive. If anyone's going to drive angry it sure as hell won't be you." I had a feeling Reggae was going to give me a big lecture on the way to the sports bar, I knew this because I could see it in his eyes that he was channeling Louis Gossett Jr.

"GOD DAMMIT ACE YOU REALLY NEED TO LEARN HOW TO CONTROL YOUR EMOTIONS! WHETHER HAMILTON GOT THROUGH TO YOU OR NOT YOU ARE GOING TO LISTEN TO WHAT I HAVE TO SAY." Before Reggae could get another word in I made the mistake of interrupting him. "Oh please Reggae if you only knew about Martinez." I only made things worse. "ARE YOU SAYING THERE IS SOMETHING I DON'T KNOW ABOUT MARTINEZ? I GET THE FEELING YOU ARE ABOUT TO SAY THAT YOU KNOW MORE THAN ME EVEN THOUGH I HAVE WELL OVER THIRTY YEARS ON YOU, AM I RIGHT?" "No sir, I would never take it that far. I only said those things to you out of frustration, I'm sorry."

"Apology accepted Ace, I hope you didn't take me yelling at you personally. I just want

to make sure that you stay on the force and avoid trouble. I look at you and see that you are

real confident in yourself. Besides, you have accomplished quite a bit for someone who has

only been on the force for a little under a year. I'm not the only one who see's it either.

However don't believe in your own hype that can become dangerous." That was some advice I

had received from one of my college professors. "Hey uh Reggae?" I said pointing to the

entrance of the sports bar. "While I'm still young?"

As we sat down at our table we talked back and forth while looking over our menus. Our

conversations shifted from one topic to another, we both made the wise decision to avoid

talking about work. And why not? We deserved a break from harsh reality for at least a little

while. "Tell me Ace, what are some of your hobbies?" "Well, weightlifting first of all. I'm also

into hiking, swimming, indoor rock climbing, and wave runners." "Oh so you like the water huh

Ace? I own private property in Colorado, big lake in the backyard with a nice view of the

Mountains. I ought to take you fishing with me one of these days." Reggae sounded real proud

of the property he owned, I could see it in his eyes. "Reggae not to change the subject but I was

wondering, do you have a wife and kids?"

The smile on his face slowly faded as he spoke. "My wife Lily passed away years ago

while giving birth to our second child. Our first born was a girl, her name is Amy she now lives in

Ohio and she is a lawyer. We see each other a few times out of the year." "What about your

second child Reggae?" "My son was a different story Ace. His name was Tommy he dropped out

of school at age fifteen and he ran away from home. I did everything I could to reach him but it

didn't do any good. I remember one night I had to work a late shift and patrol an apartment

complex on the wrong side of the tracks. Around this time of night the cars that belonged to the residents of this apartment would end up vandalized and in some cases stolen.

Well I was getting ready to go home when I noticed someone wearing a ski mask

suspiciously looking inside various cars. When I got close enough to him I drew my gun and told

him to put his hands up. Instead he reached in his front pocket and pulled out a gun. Before he

had a chance to aim I fired three shots and hit him square in his chest. I walked over to examine

him. He wasn't moving so I knew for a fact that he was dead. I removed his ski mask and saw

that it was Tommy. I called for an ambulance and just sat down and stared at his lifeless body.

Even though he would have killed me his death still haunts me. Despite the atrocities and

horrors I had experienced in Vietnam this one shook me hard." "Reggae I'm sorry, I didn't mean

to pry." "No Ace its really ok. However while were here I want you to promise me something,

don't let this job get to you. Uphold the law, reinforce traditional values, fight for what's right but don’t break down on me. You have come such a long way so just keep moving forward.

And for the love of God will you please order something? I’m hungry dammit!” I went with my usual diet of burgers and fries while Reggae just ate soup and salad. It was two for one on drinks that night so Reggae and I agreed to call a taxi cab and have the police cruiser towed for when we were ready to leave. Before we knew it we had gone through about four beers in no time. “Ace I’m impressed, I appreciate you a lot more when you are drunk. You’re a real asshole when you’re sober.” I laughed and said “Reggae, drinking makes dealing with you less painful.” Reggae and I continued to exchange laughter, I don’t drink too often but I really needed this. I love my job and have strong desires to be a hero but I still wanted to feel human and enjoy life.

“I don’t know about you Reggae but I think we should call it a night.” “Ace its only eight o’clock. Are you sure you only had four drinks? Come on junior, don’t let this old man give you a reason to make fun of you on Monday." I decided to drink two more with Reggae. "I am going to feel like shit in the morning Ace, but at least I won't be the only one." We stuck around until about nine and then headed toward the parking lot. We had no problem getting a taxi and a tow truck. As soon as I got home I fell face first on my couch and passed out. Before I knew it morning had arrived and I had the biggest headache. I popped a few pills and went back to bed, I finally woke up at around noon. I was still feeling a little sick but better than I did earlier that morning. I checked my phone and sure enough someone had left me a message, I only hoped it had nothing to do with work. I was relieved when I realized it was my dad who had left me a message asking me to meet him and Mom for dinner. I was more than happy to take him up on that offer.

I met up with Mom and Dad that evening at Outback Steakhouse. Spending time with my parents was always a pleasure, I was still close with them even after all these years. "So son

how's work going for you?" "Honestly Dad it has its ups and downs, some ways it is a peaceful

easy feeling knowing that I am removing offenders from the streets and on the other hand it is

frustrating when our courts either put them back on the streets. Both Mom and Dad looked at

me with remorse because I knew for a fact that they felt my pain. "But enough about that Dad,

how's retirement treating you?" Dad had been retired from Hillsborough County Tax Collectors

Office for a little while now, as I could see him and Mom were making the most of it. Rightfully

so, Dad had worked real hard over the years to support Mom and I. Overall I could tell that

Mom and Dad were both happy and content.

"Son retirement is going great for the both of us when you get some time off you should

join Mom and I for a road trip or something to take your mind off the frustrations of your job."

"Ace honey you should really take your fathers advice. Not only that but we don't see you enough as it is." Exclaimed my mother. "Mom Dad I have no objection to your offers

whatsoever. However its about that time for the bill and don't worry this one is on me."

"Well son thank you for dinner, hope you pay for our meals more often." Laughed my father.

"Bye sweetheart." Said Mom as I embraced her and my father before going our separate ways

for the evening.

The very next morning I went to the gym to get in a quick workout. Today was chest day

and even though that is my favorite workout it took me the longest. I was especially wasting

time in the gym today because all I could think about was my meeting with Hamilton in the

morning. Hamilton wasn't angry with me but I was still worried, what kind of dirt was he going

to dig up on my other co-workers? Whatever it was I kept telling myself to be brave and face

whatever challenges he might have for me. As I was getting ready to start me second set of incline bench presses Jerry the gyms owner interrupted my train of thought with a small joke.

"Ace, I know you like the sight of your own reflection but eventually you will have to let

someone else use this bench." I looked at him and laughed for a little bit. I'm actually glad he

came along when he did because I was starting to think I had no sense of humor.

"You know Jerry you are a real smartass however if you don't mind a real man is trying

to workout here." It didn't stop there, before he went on about his day he was going to have

the last word. "Well Ace if you want to even be close to my league you'd better get back to

work." We laughed back and forth for a bit then we said our goodbyes. It took a while but I did

finish my workout. When I arrived home from the gym I decided to stay home and relax for the

rest of the day.

The next morning I anxiously made my way to Hamilton's office, I couldn't wait any

longer for the news he was going to give me. "Ok Captain who else needs to be straightened out in this department?" "Get comfortable McMillan you are going to be here for a while this is

a pretty good sized list." I took a seat and Hamilton dropped a decent sized stack of papers in

front of me. "Let me guess more paper work?" "No" laughed Hamilton. "These are some of the

other deputies that need to be off my force but thanks to powers beyond me and Chief

Lawrence's control keep avoiding termination." I looked through the different files and saw the

faces of six different officers one of them was Martinez. I didn't have to read his file since I

knew by experience he was bad news in addition to Hamilton giving me vital information about

his track record. "Ace the reason why the paper work is so thick is because these folks have

major skeletons in their closets. You already know about Martinez so I'll start with the

remaining five.

First we have David Corso, David had a habit of roughing up inmates in the jails. Even if they were just petty offenders. His only disciplinary action was paid leave and a job transfer

working the streets. Next we have Kyle Bradford, Kyle was off duty when he had committed his

offense. He pulled out his gun and fired at a twelve year old buy all because the kid stole a bag

of chips. Not a single person was hit with his gun fire and all he got was a week suspension

without pay and was forced to attend anger management. Moving right along here's Bruce

Jacobs. Bruce was banned from a baseball stadium in the Pinellas County area for being drunk

and disorderly. He avoided arrest but was permanently banned from the stadium and received

harsh reprimand from internal affairs.

Our fourth offender was caught on dash cam during her escapade. Take a good look at

this video Ace you are probably thinking to yourself big deal she is just cuffing and patting down

a drunk driver. As you can see here she uses his hands to rub her crotch. She tried to smooth

things over by saying he was the instigator. Oh before I forget her name is Linda Michaels and her only penalties were paid administrative leave and writing a letter of apology to the man and his family. Last but not least we have Gary Matthews. Matthews was called to break up a domestic dispute between a man and his wife. He did as he was told but he used extreme force in the process. He beat and bruised the couple with his nightstick. He was tried and taken to court. Although the couple filed a restraining order against Matthews he was still able to avoid jail time and termination. Ace aside from the offenses these officers committed as individuals, they did commit one of their crimes as a group."

Hamilton showed me another video. "Be strong Ace you are not going to like this." It turned out Martinez and the other five officers were caught on video a few years ago aggressively attacking a youthful offender. They took turns beating and choking him. One of the officers forced pills down his throat. I remember seeing this on the news and the outrage of the public when no charges were filed against the six officers. "Captain I have to ask, how

come when you and the chief fire bad cops how come they keep getting rehired?" "Ace here's

the deal, these officers are rehired because of the panel." "Who makes up the panel Captain?"

"Ace the panel consists of two cops, and the district attorney.

Remember when I told you I couldn't have my officers taking the law into their own

hands?" "Yes Captain I remember." "Ace I take it all back, you have been working here for

nearly a year now, you have more than earned my trust. This force needs to be cleaned up, I

would do it myself but I'm too old to carry out such deeds. Ace I need you to do

something very important. I need you to kill these particular officers! You don't have to do it

today or tomorrow but it has to be done. If you are worried about covering your tracks I will

supply you with weapons, here is a spare key to the evidence locker. Be organized with the killings don't kill them all at once kill one or two and give yourself a cooling off period. Do your best to make it look as though street thugs had killed those bastards. I can see it now Ace things are going be different around here."

I left work that day feeling quite anxious. It was exciting, I felt like a hero in some action movie who was going to save the day. However I decided not to pursue this mission right away I wanted to take some time to plan strategies and study my targets. So for the next few weeks I did my usual work routines, filled out paper work, wrote tickets, made various arrests, and occasionally got together with Reggae outside of work. Before I knew it I had been with the force for exactly one year, I had scored a great amount of vacation time, and I was promoted to sergeant. A few days after my promotion Reggae insisted that I use up some of my vacation time. He called me over to his house, he said he had big news for me.

"Ace remember when I told you that I have property in Colorado?" "Oh yeah Reggae I remember it well." "I am going to visit my property to do some fishing and to escape Florida for

a little while. One more thing you are coming with me!" "Reggae I appreciate this but what

about plane tickets and flight scheduling?" "Ace don't worry I'm flying us! I was a pilot in

Vietnam and I own a small plane." The next morning a taxi picked us up and we were taken to a

hangar in the Zephyrhills area. Within no time we touched down near a well decorated cabin

next to a good sized lake. As soon as I got out I took my time to become acquainted with my

surroundings. "Reggae this is unbelievable, I have only seen places like this is magazines or on

television." "Ace my boy we are going to be here for a little bit let's take our stuff inside

and eat breakfast."

After a nice big breakfast Reggae and I went hiking through the woods. We didn't dare

tread through the forest without bringing a few guns however. I kept reminding myself I was no longer in Tampa and that nature truly had the upper hand. Thankfully we had no deadly encounters whatsoever. Upon our return to the cabin Reggae fired up the boat and we went off to do some fishing. Although I wasn't a huge fan of fishing I was real glad to be here, in a boat surrounded by nature and with a good friend. Reggae caught a decent amount of lake trout as for me I caught about one or two mountain white fish. After we became bored with fishing Reggae and I sat back and admired the area. "Reggae I don't understand this area is so peaceful, have you ever considered retiring and just living here? Don't get me wrong I'd hate to see you go but this seems like an ideal retirement spot." Reggae smiled and said to me "Well Ace if I retire I wouldn't get to train young punks like yourself. Besides I inherited this land from my great grand daddy I was going to give it to my son and daughter but with him out of the picture this will all belong to Amy someday."

"Well I am sure she would appreciate that, you seem like you are a hell of a father." At that moment Reggaes smile didn't seem as big. "Well it's too bad I could never reach my son, I

lost a lot of good friends in Vietnam and I had to hand flags to quite a few widows and children

but I will always grieve over the fact that I killed my own son. I know he would have killed me

but it just hurts Ace." "I have no children of my own Reggae but again I understand why you are

upset, would you like me to talk about something else?" Reggae smiled and nodded. "Ace tell

me some stories. Talk about whatever you want, girls, weightlifting, 80s hair metal I don't care.

"Well in case you didn't already know I listen to 80s hair metal while working out."

"I never would have imagined" Reggae said sarcastically.

After swapping stories back and forth Reggae and I headed back to shore. By the time

we made it back it was early afternoon and Reggae threw a few steaks on the grill. While

waiting for our steaks we drank beer, arm wrestled, and played a few games of checkers.

Despite the fact that Reggae hadn't lifted weights in a number of years he managed to beat me in arm wrestling. Around that time he decided to tell me "Oh by the way Ace, I used to do competitive arm wrestling, I even have a few trophies." I laughed and shook my head, "Reggae just get the steaks and knock off the trash talk." "I have to say Ace I'm really glad you came here with me, and also you have really loosened up throughout the time we have worked together, you may not have a heart attack at age forty after all." I laughed so hard that I spit beer out of my nose. For the next twenty minutes I sat down and laughed real hard so hard in fact I didn't eat my steak right away.

After I finally stopped laughing Reggae had a serious talk with me about my change of character. "All kidding aside Ace I really meant those things that I said to you, you are a hell of a guy and I think you being here with me has been real good therapy for you." I smiled and raised my bottle to Reggae. "Reggae thank you again for bringing me here, I hope you and me have a lot of good years on the force together." After lunch we decided to take a trail up the

mountains. We were so high up we practically touched the clouds. This whole experience made

me wish I had taken a vacation out of Florida sooner. I knew that I should enjoy my time in

Colorado but I couldn't help but dread going back to Florida.

On top of that, the mission that Hamilton wanted me to carry out. Was I really capable

of such an accomplishment? Would it really make a difference? "ACE!" "What is it Reggae?" I

said in a startled tone. "Are you done daydreaming or what? Its getting late we need to get

back to the cabin." As we made our way down the mountain trail I strictly focused on what was

going on right here and now, especially because I didn't want Reggae to catch me daydreaming.

Upon our return to the cabin I went through a few messages on my phone, I took my time

getting back to those who had called me. Besides, how soon would I get to visit Colorado again?

Back at the cabin Reggae and I had spaghetti for dinner, probably a good idea seeing as how it was getting late and we planned on coming back to Tampa the next day. The next morning we gathered our material and headed back home.

For the remainder of my vacation I hung out with friends and family. The following Monday evening when I returned to work Reggae and I had to pair up with Martinez and a few other deputies, according to Martinez an anonymous tipster gave information about a crack house somewhere in College Hill. Reggae and I got in my cruiser and followed Martinez and the others. We stood outside the house for a little while and waited for the signal from our inside informant. Martinez, Reggae, and myself waited by the front door while the other members of our team waited in the back. Seconds later we made our entrance and were greeted by seven men who were ready to shoot us no matter what the cost. Martinez fired and successfully killed one of the dealers hitting right between his eyes. Reggae and I followed and tore through five more offenders. The last thug standing never had a chance to fire his gun he put down his piece

and raised both hands in the air surrendering.

We slowly approached him and called in the other deputies. They held him down cuffed

him and read him his rights. Before they hauled him off to jail that night he informed us there

was one more person in the house. Two of our people searched the rest of the house while the

others escorted the cuffed individual to his cruiser. Meanwhile I stayed with Reggae and

Martinez. The two officers that had searched the remainder of the house said they found no

one. At that moment we heard shots ring out in the backyard. I went with Martinez and Reggae

while the other two stayed behind us.

As we hopped fences I kept thinking more and more that our last member had evaded

us, we had even lost sight of Martinez. Reggae and I told the two deputies accompanying us to

go home for the night. Reggae and I eventually caught up with Martinez he had the suspect up against the wall. I was getting ready to declare this a job well done but instead something else

happened. Martinez aimed his gun at Reggae and fired, Reggae fell down instantly the bullet

had hit him just a few inches from his heart. I dove to ground and embraced Reggae begging

him not to die. I grabbed my radio and called for backup. "OFFICER DOWN OFFICER DOWN

BRING AN AMBULANCE!" At that moment Martinez and his friend taunted me and laughed at

me. "Well asshole it looks like you and me are even. Ace I want you to meet my friend Jesse,

Jesse and I have been planning this for quite a while now. You may have beaten me in a fight

and stolen my promotion but I just ruined your life." "You lost Ace!" Laughed Jesse.

At that moment Reggae spoke to me in a soft voice. "Ace, listen to me I'm not going to

make it but don't let my death ruin you. Be brave and keep wearing your badge, you will get

through this." At that moment Reggae had died. The ambulance finally arrived but it made no difference, the most important person outside of my friends and family was gone. That night I didn't sleep I laid in bed mourning the loss of my friend. The very next day I went to work, tired and angry. Hamilton made it clear he didn't want me working that day. "Ace go home, I'm sorry about last night but I don't expect you to work in your current condition." "Captain, it's my fault that Reggae is gone I owe him. And another thing, Martinez killed him."

"I had a feeling it was him, I tried calling his phone he won't answer. For all we know he is hiding out. Take care of Martinez when you have recovered. One more thing Ace, Reggae's funeral is in two days." I left Hamilton's office and decided to try and get some rest.

Two days later I attended Reggaes funeral, I was surrounded by co-workers and family. My parents held me close during my hour of need and told me how sorry they were. Martinez was nowhere in sight he wasn't as dumb as I thought he was. Minutes later a young black woman approached the podium. It was Reggaes daughter Amy, she spent the next five minutes talking about Reggae, how he was a great father and role model. After the service had ended the police force had rented out a lobby at a hotel. I gave Amy my condolences and told her how Reggae spoke very highly of her. She smiled and hugged me and started to tell some of the stories Reggae told her about me. “You know Ace my father really loved his job and he told me all about you and how you were fun to work with. I hope you don’t quit after what happened, after the way my dad talked about you it would be wrong for you to leave the force. Before you go Ace my dad gave me these he wants you to have them and don’t say no.”

It was a pair of dog tags bearing Reggaes name. “Thank you Amy, please make it home safely I hope I see you again.” We embraced and said our goodbyes, I headed home to grieve in private and hopefully get some rest. I laid in bed crying all alone for my friend and mentor had been taken from me. I held his dog tags close to my chest and failed to fight back tears of rage. I

would eventually lay the dog tags on my nightstand and drift off to sleep. Surprisingly I started

to dream, I was walking around various parts of Tampa only it was quiet and every building and

house I walked by was dilapidated and run down. I was waiting to hear the sound of cars

however the silence continued. My surroundings symbolized how I felt inside; alone. Standing

before me was an abandoned warehouse something told me to go inside and take a look

around.

I walked around for a while almost as if someone was going to emerge from the

dark shadows in the corners of the empty building. Suddenly a figure came out of the darkness

and walked toward me, it was Reggae. "It's good to see you Ace, take Amy's advice and stay on

the force." I ran to Reggae and hugged him and told him how sorry I was for his death. "Reggae

I could have prevented this, it's my fault you are here." "Ace my death was not your fault, besides I know about you and Hamilton, you have a mission to carry out. You are so close you

can't lose now." Soon we were joined by another guest, I saw a light gleaming in the darkness.

It was a badge, it was attached to a police uniform being worn by a skeleton.

I watched in horror as the corpse like being approached me and placed his hand on my

shoulder while staring at me with his glowing red eyes and permanent sadistic grin. "Don't be

afraid Ace, he's only here to encourage you. Pick up where he left off and kill them all!" I woke

up covered in sweat. I looked at the clock and saw that it was only 2:00 in the morning, I was

always told that nothing good ever happens after that time I was going to make that a reality

for someone before the sun came up. I threw on a pair of jeans, a shirt, and Reggaes dog tags

then I jumped in my car.

I went back to the scene of Reggaes death to retrace my steps. I decided to test my luck and use my radio to see if I could track Martinez's radio. This was a trick that Reggae had shown

me when teaching me about police radios. Sure enough he was close by. I followed the signal

and traced it to a beat up house located On Florida Avenue near the Hillsborough River. I

parked my car not too far from the house. The odds were in my favor since I moved real slow

on top of that I was driving my Impala not my cruiser. I peered into the front window of the

house and saw something I didn't expect; it was Jesse holding Martinez's radio. I kicked the

door open and shot Jesse in his leg, he screamed in agony.

"Where's Martinez Jesse?" "I don't know Ace." "MARTINEZ!" I repeated as I forcefully

pressed my shoe into his wound. "Okay Ace I'll talk, he said something about getting his friends

together and taking back what should have been his. I will tell him whatever you want just hear

me out please."

I pointed my gun to his face and he stared back at me with fear and anxiety in his eyes.

"There's an easier way for you to deliver my message Jesse." "How's that Ace?" "In death!" I fired twice at his chest and one at his head. I poured bleach on Jesse and around various areas over the floors of the house then I threw Jesses body in my trunk. I drove my car to I-75 and headed south. As I was coming close to the Gibsonton exit I parked my car to the far right side of the bridge over the Alafia River. I threw Jesses bleach covered corpse off the bridge and into the river.

I headed back north from there, as I drove back toward my home my heart was racing, I wasn't scared or nervous for once I was actually proud of myself for wrecking life. Besides which, everyone that I was after deserved to die! Even though I wanted to take down a few more on the way home I decided to go back home and try to get some rest. As day hit I checked my phone to see if any co-workers had tried to reach me. I did get a voicemail from Hamilton telling me how I needed to swing by work later in the day to supervise an employee. Apparently this guy was on his ninety day probation period and I had to ride along with him. I showed up to

work at around 6pm I was actually looking forward to playing teacher.

The person I had to supervise however clearly didn't want to be there. His name was

Harold Martin, he used to be a sergeant in the New Port Richey area but was demoted by a

unanimous vote due to his anger issues. And if that wasn't bad enough he had over twenty

years on me. We hung around the Barnes N Noble parking lot on Dale Mabry in the Carrollwood

area waiting to catch a bad driver or two. Sure enough somebody just missed a yellow light

Martin and I raced toward him and pulled him over at the parking lot of an orthodontists office.

Harold approached the drivers vehicle and followed the usual procedures. Asking for license,

registration, and insurance. He came back to the cruiser to run the young man's information.

"What was his response to why he was pulled over?" I asked curiously. "Well Ace he admitted to running a red light but I am going to have a little talk with him."

I stepped out of the cruiser to do some stretching but also to keep an eye on Harold. I

would soon learn about Harold's anger issues for something bad was about to happen. "Sir step

out of the vehicle." This clearly wasn't necessary in my book especially since the driver

admitted his error. Harold's behavior wouldn't stop there however. "Turn around! Lean against

the vehicle with your hands above your head." Harold proceeded to aggressively pat down the

driver at that moment. Finally I couldn't take it anymore, I grabbed Martin by his hair walked

him over to the cruiser and slammed his face into the hood of the cruiser. I pulled him back up

and repeatedly punched his face. In the midst of it all I told the driver to leave the scene and

drive safe. I continued my assault on Martin, I wanted him to remember this day. I would then

force his hands behind his back to cuff him. "Officer Martin, you are under arrest for police

brutality, and if I catch you bullying anyone I'll kill you!"

I drove us back to headquarters and believe it or not he had very little to say to me. I

yanked him out of the backseat and walked him into Hamilton's office. I sat him down in

the office and waited to hear the captains thoughts about this incident.

"So Ace what did you do this time?" "Well Captain I'd say that I solved a problem today.

You see Martin over here pulled over a teenage boy for running a red light he then told him to

step out of the vehicle at that point he became aggressive with the driver and started yelling at

him." At that point I removed Martins badge and placed it on Hamilton's desk. "I know about

your track record Harold you should have been taken off the force a long time ago."

"Martin is all of this true?" "Yes sir it was all caught on my dash cam." Replied Harold in

an embarrassed tone. "Ace get him out of my sight. Officer Harold Martin you are hereby

terminated from my force, too bad you have to learn the hard way that there is no favoritism in my force." As I walked toward the exit Harold and I were stopped by one of the more attractive

female deputies. Her name was Holly Brooks, and she wasn't going to let me step out that

quickly. "Hi Ace, where are you going?" "Excuse us Holly I have to transport this gentleman to

Olson Road Jail. After that I am going to patrol the streets for the rest of the night."

"Oh Ace you never take the day off do you? You are practically married to this job." She

threw her arms around me and pressed me up against her large breasts. I looked at her pretty

face and her long red hair. She was the kind of woman I was attracted to but with my change of

personality and disconnection that I had been feeling I would make no effort to make her my

girlfriend. "Holly I will get back to you another time I have to get to the jail I'll see you later."

On the way to the jail Harold had nothing to say to me. Which didn't bother me at all I

just wanted him behind bars and cut off from society.

After I left the jail I headed to Perkins on Fowler Avenue for a quick meal. I was hungry and I wanted to take some time to sit down and clear my head. The food was good as usual

it wasn't the same without Reggae. Even though I was keeping my promise to clean things

up I still missed Reggae. His death truly shattered my world I just hope I can live up to the

promises I had made. I checked my phone and it was now 11pm, I wanted to head back home

but judging by the talk on my police radio my services were needed. "Sergeant McMillan you

are needed at The Travelers Inn on Busch Boulevard, we received word about a sexual assault

involving a young woman between the ages of thirty-five and forty." "I'm on my way."

I wasted no time driving toward the location, not the greatest part of town but I knew

this mess had to be cleaned up. When I arrived on the scene all I saw was a fellow police officer

talking to a man in the leasing office who was clearly embarrassed to be there. In the parking

lot I saw a woman making a scene pointing her finger toward the man in the office. She had no visible injuries and she didn't appear the least bit upset. "Miss what is your name and what

seems to be the problem?" "Well Officer my name is Katie and I want you to arrest the man

inside the leasing office, he kidnapped me and raped me in room 201." "Ok Katie hang tight out

here for a minute I am going to speak with the officer inside."

"Hello Sergeant McMillan my name is Officer Tom Parker how are you?" "I'm doing well

what seems to be the trouble here tonight?" "Well this young man right here had a one night

stand with the young lady outside, she got angry when he didn't want to be her boyfriend so

she cried rape. I searched their motel room and all I found was a used condom the sex was

clearly sensual." "Thanks Tom I can take it from here, sir what's your name?" "I'm Andrew sir."

"Ok Andrew how are you feeling are you going to make it home safely tonight?" "Yes sir I think I

will manage." "Well Andrew I only ask because I have had this happen to me before I know how upsetting it can be." After sending Andrew on his way I wanted to have a long talk with Katie.

"Miss come here for a second, I need to see you license." I ran her information through my computer and saved her information, I was going to use it for later. "Katie I don't know what you were trying to pull tonight but you could have ruined that young man's life. In fact I am giving you an order to appear in court tomorrow morning in front of a judge. As of tonight you will head straight home is that understood?" "Yes sir thank you." I watched her leave little did she know I was going to pay her a visit within the next few hours. Despite the great teachings Reggae had instilled in me I still had a grudge toward women who fake rape.

Around one o'clock in the morning I decided to pay Katie a little visit. I left my sirens off so I wouldn't distract cars passing by. The lights were on and she was in her living room watching television. I knocked on her door and she answered right away. "Officer what brings you here tonight?" I responded by kicking her in the chest and watching her fall flat on her back. She rolled over on her chest and desperately crawled toward her telephone I slowly made my way into her house put on a pair of gloves shut the door behind me and locked it. I walked toward the right side of her body and kicked her in the ribs.

She rolled back over on her back howling in pain. I lifted her off the floor by her hair and used my right fist to get in a few good punches to her face. I then threw onto the floor and watched her cry in the corner begging me to stop. I would have said something to her but what was the point? She didn't care about the hurt she had caused others so I aimed my gun at her forehead and fired. I followed the same procedure with her as I did after killing Jesse, only I hid her body in a different location. I headed south on 56th street and disposed of her body over the bridge and into the Hillsborough River.

After completing one of my many personal vendettas I decided to call it a night. I raced home wondering how long it would be until someone filled out a missing persons report for

Katie and Jesse? As much as I wanted to believe no one would miss trash like them I knew

certain people would ask such questions. Another thing that had been plaguing my mind was

why a skeleton dressed as a police officer had visited me in my dreams? Even though I had only

seen him that one time something about him seemed so familiar. One thing was for sure,

Reggae insisted that I pick up where he left off. Whether I found out who the ghoulish being

was or not all I knew was that I had to carry out my purpose.

Later that morning I went to the cemetery to visit Reggaes tombstone. I wanted to talk

to him alone there was so much I wanted to tell him. "Reggae I am thankful to have had the

pleasure to work with you. I know I have the support of the captain but I am out here on my

own I wish you were here. Someday you and me will be sitting back sharing laughs again however that will be a while because I have a lot of work to do." I left the cemetery and headed

toward the police station on the way there I cranked up the radio and played a few of my

favorite songs. Songs that appeared on soundtracks to various 80s movies, these particular

songs would usually be played while the hero is flashing back to the good times he had with a

recently deceased loved one.

I used to have a friend who made fun of me when I would play this music when he rode

with me in my car. His name was Jason, and even though this was an emotional time for me, it

would have been nice to have him here. He was a good guy but I sometimes get the feeling that

he wouldn't want to see me this way. He and I grew up together admiring the tough but

depressed burnt out cops we saw in various action movies. Unfortunately this was real life and

after my recent experiences almost nothing could ease my pain. Friends and family insisted that

I talk to a professional but I kept making excuses. I know it's not healthy but I wanted to hold on to the anger and contempt I felt toward my enemies, I was in a certain state of mind and I was

afraid that treatment would cause me to lose my drive.

As I left the cemetery I received a phone call from Hamilton, apparently it was an urgent

matter so I wasted no time in heading toward the station. It seemed like it was business

as usual when I walked in the building, co-workers running around handling paper work and

tending to offenders. In the midst of the restless crowd I saw Hamilton standing in front of his

office motioning me to come in and have a seat. "Have a seat Sergeant. So tell me Ace what has

been going on these past few weeks?" "Well captain it's been difficult I still grieve over losing

Reggae." "McMillan I am going to cut right to the chase, what do you know about an individual

by the name of Jesse?" "Well Captain I know that he is dead and in no time at all Martinez is

going to come looking for me."

"What does Jesse have to do with Martinez?" "Captain he was involved in Reggaes death." Hamilton sat silently in his seat for a few seconds and starred at me. "GOD DAMMIT

MCMILLAN WHY DIDN'T YOU INFORM ME SOONER? BOTH THE CHIEF OF POLICE AND THE

MAYOR ARE ON MY ASS ABOUT THIS ONE I OUGHT TO PHYSICALLY TOSS YOU OUT THAT DOOR

RIGHT NOW!" "Now Captain if you do that who's going to take my place? It sure as hell won't

be you." "Very well McMillan you've made your point. Before you go Reggae made a

special request. Sergeant Ace McMillan I hereby promote you to Lieutenant."

I saluted Hamilton and told him thank you. "Ace before you go here is a bag I want

you to go into the evidence locker and pick up a few items just make sure you pick up the

weapons that have already been used during past trials." As I made my way toward the

evidence locker I was approached by a familiar face, it was Martinez and boy did he look angry.

He stood in front of me and put his hand on my chest. "Listen Ace you'd better not rat me out, I know you are responsible for Jesses death so were going to make ourselves a little deal, you

keep your mouth shut about Reggaes death and maybe I'll let you walk." No sooner did he

finish talking trash I grabbed him by his shirt picked him up to make an example out of him.

"Listen to me Martinez you refer to me as Lieutenant McMillan from here on out is that clear?"

Martinez trembled within my grasp and responded to me in a most cowardly tone. "Yes

sir it won't happen again?" After letting go of Martinez I decided to get everyone else's

attention. "EVERYONE STOP WHAT YOU ARE DOING I HAVE AN ANNOUNCEMENT TO MAKE.

WHEN YOU WALK OUT OF THIS BUILDING TODAY REMEMBER WHO YOU ARE WORKING FOR,

WHO YOU ARE PROTECTING AND THE IDEALS YOU ARE REINFORCING. IF YOU BREAK ANY OF

THESE RULES YOU WILL END UP LIKE MARTINEZ." My stern lecture was met with praise

Martinez however was hit with a barrage of laughter from his colleagues.

As I walked into the evidence locker I saw all sorts of neat toys. Quite a few of these

were not even legal for regular street cops to carry. My eyes lit up like a child on Christmas day

when I saw a pair of ooze's especially because they had already been used in a trial from five

years ago. I also found a double barrel shotgun along with a bazooka and box of grenades.

Wasn't sure whether or not the grenades were duds I took the box because I figured I'd never

know unless I tried. I took the items home with me and went through the list of people I was

told to kill.

I wasn't exactly sure who I wanted to start with but I had decided early on that Martinez

was going to die last. After careful consideration I decided to go after Corso for starters.

First I had to go back to the station to check the schedules of my victims. Corso had to work a

late shift and since I was now Lieutenant I had the authority to call my own hours.

Corso was scheduled to be on Sheldon road that night and I was going to do my best to ruin his night. I'll be damned if he was going to stay on this force. Before heading toward Corso's

location I stopped at a convenient store somewhere on Bruce B Downs to buy a few six packs of

beer.

Since Corso was a fellow colleague I knew that I would really have to cover my tracks. As

I headed west on Hillsborough avenue to Sheldon Road in my Impala I called Corso on his radio

and told him to head a few miles north on Sheldon and meet me near one of the ditches. He

headed to the requested location without question and waited for me. I arrived at half past

midnight. I approached his vehicle and he stepped out. I kindly struck up a small conversation

with him to lure him into a false since of security.

"So Corso I understand that due to your behavior in the jail they transferred you to the

streets?" "Lieutenant what is this all about?" "Corso I am only getting to know you, is it also

true that you and five other officers were involved in the death of a youthful offender in a boot camp?" "Yes Ace that is true but I hope you know we were found not guilty. Besides you may

have authority over me but you are not the law." At this point I realized that I was getting a rise

out of him so I decided to cut to the chase. I raised my gun to him and asked him about

Martinez. "Alright Corso stop wasting my time, what is your connection with Martinez and what

is he planning?"

Corso's face turned white as a ghost as he reached for the sky. "Okay Ace lets take it

easy, you know I wasn't involved in Reggae's death." "That maybe so Corso but I know that you

him and the other four are close friends." "The truth is Martinez never liked you or Reggae, and

to see you excel in the force the way that you have twisted him up inside and he decided that

he had to get back at you by killing Reggae. Another thing when you go home at night check

your neighborhood for any suspicious people he did mention wanting to take you out when you are least expecting it." "Thanks a lot Corso before I leave tonight you need to do one last thing

for me." "Ace I'll do whatever you say just please let me live." That was the moment I decided

to bring out the six pack of beer I had purchased earlier that night. Little did he know I wasn't

going to let him leave this area alive.

"Get in your cruiser turn it toward the ditch and put it in park. Now as long as I have this

gun pointed at you, you will keep drinking." "Ace this is blackmail." I put the gun closer to his

head and demanded him to drink. He went through his first bottle pretty quickly then I handed

him another. Soon he went through for beers at this point I started taunting him. "Don't worry

Corso, with you track record the bosses will go easy on you for being drunk on the job." Before

he had a chance to insult me I hit him over the head with the butt end of my gun. He was

knocked unconscious with his head resting on the steering wheel I reached in and put his

cruiser in drive. I watched it slowly crash to the bottom of the ditch and explode.

I immediately jumped into my car and headed north. Lucky for me there was little to

no traffic on the road. Within no time at all the fire department was on the scene hopefully

they would not suspect another person was involved in this matter. I decided to quit while I was

ahead for the evening Hamilton and I agreed that it was best to cover my tracks.

The next morning however it was all over the news. Unfortunately for them they didn't have

too much material to run with especially because all they found were charred remains of the

vehicle and Corso's body. The department decided to rule Corso's death as a suicide and move

on.

With Corso out of the picture I started to feel more in control of my destiny. However I

decided to wait and carefully plan my next kill. For the next two weeks it was business as usual,

training new deputies, making busts, writing tickets, and filling out series after series of paper work. After my two week waiting period I decided that Linda would be next on my hit list. I took

a look at her schedule for the week and made a mental note as to when I should track her

location. She was scheduled to work Tuesday night north on Nebraska Avenue near the

intersection of Bearss.

I went to the station after hours so I could shop in the evidence locker without having to

look over my shoulder. I browsed for a few minutes hoping to find a weapon that would finish

the job quickly. Sure enough I was able to find a sniper rifle, there were other items I wanted to

take home but I knew I would be back soon enough to claim said material. Around 11:30 that

evening Linda had her cruiser parked on the north end of Nebraska anxiously awaiting drivers

to speed or run through a red light. I was heading north on Florida Avenue at the time. I wanted

to make sure that Linda did not see me at all. Before Florida and Nebraska merged to form one

road I turned left on the intersection behind a Publix Grocery Store. I made a right hand turn and headed south on Nebraska for part of the way. I saw Linda's cruiser from a distance and made a left turn on Sinclair Hills.

Near this intersection was a large parking lot with two small buildings that had been out of business for quite sometime. It was poorly lit so I knew I could make a fast get away after taking down Linda. I parked in a dark area near an old abandoned warehouse and set up my scope. I watched Linda stand by her car near the road holding a radar gun. I fired a clear shot and hit her just above her left ear. I didn't dare stick around to see the aftermath so I jumped in my car and headed east on Sinclair Hills. I decided to hide out in Pasco County for the evening so I headed north on Livingston as soon as I reached the end of Sinclair Hills.

I made it to a hotel in Zephyrhills at around 12:30. I was able to find a room with no trouble whatsoever. I immediately turned on the television so I could watch the news. Believe it or not everyone was on the scene not too long after I had killed Deputy Linda Michaels.

According to the report after the bullet struck the left side of her head her corpse fell onto the

street and was run over by a car. Reporters also said how there was no suspects at the time but

that police were actively searching the killer. Even though I respect the men and women of law

enforcement this report further proved the fact that when a cop dies everyone is on the case

however when a civilian dies very little effort is made in seeking out the individual responsible

for the wrong doing.

I laid in bed reminding myself that there were only four left and that after them I would

take on the panel. I went to bed and as I felt myself drift off to sleep I began to dream. Only it

wasn't a pleasant dream, it was a further decent into madness. I dreamt that I was taking

multiple lives in short periods of time, some were civilians others were men and women who

had disrespected the badge. I was enjoying every scream and every plea for mercy on I shot, stabbed, pummeled, and torched my way through a mob of people protesting me in front of a

courthouse.

As I kicked the doors open I saw the courtroom filled with my enemies. The groups

consisted of people that I had killed, people I was planning to kill, while the remainder were

people I had seen a few hours ago on the news talking trash about how they were going to find

Linda's killer .

They all stared at me in fear especially the judge and jury. I smiled at them and proceeded to

shoot each person one at a time. As I saw the judge cringing in his seat looking down at me I

stacked corpse after corpse in front of his stand, I intended to scare him before taking his life.

When I reached his stand I stood on top of it and lifted him out of his seat by his robe. I

saw the fear in his eyes and saw the sweat run down his flesh. Before killing him I took one look

at the people outside the courtroom. They were crowds of people cheering my name supporting my deeds. I looked at the judges face and gave him a short speech to make sure he

would be traumatized even in death. “I don’t care how high I have to stack these bodies there

will be plenty of room for you among them!” Before I could end him I awoke from my sleep.

It was 9:45 in the morning and the sun shined brightly through my window, I grabbed the

phone and decided to call for room service.

Forty-five minutes later a large breakfast had arrived and as I reached for my wallet the

attendant cheerfully rejected my cash and pointed to my badge that was laying on the

nightstand. I thanked the gentleman and he went on his way. Within minutes I had devoured a

large steak with a stack of pancakes along with three eggs and three strips of bacon. Despite

last nights killing I was feeling pretty calm, not to mention there were no voice mails or texts on

my phone. Around elven o’clock in the morning I turned on the news and saw that last nights incident was still being talked about. Cops were everywhere, they had plenty of suspects in

mind however I was not among those they had suspected.

Police Chief Lawrence was questioned by various reporters on last nights killing. One

News reporter had this to say. “Chief was Linda Michaels death in any way shape or form

connected with the death of David Corso?” “Absolutely not, Corso’s death was ruled out as

suicide, there is no connection whatsoever.” The second and last news reporter didn’t do much

better. “Chief do you believe that Officer Rick Thompson is responsible for the killing of Deputy

Michaels?” “Where have you been these past few years? Rick Thompson lives outside of Florida

and supposedly he has retired, how the hell could he be a suspect? No more questions people.”

I laughed and changed the channel after seeing the chief slam a door in the reporters

face. I settled on Fox News and saw that Mayor Roland Riker was approaching the podium to

address the public. “Citizens of Tampa, although Deputy Linda Michaels death was unjust let me remind everyone that Michaels was no saint herself, a few years ago she along with Corso

and four other officers were involved in the death of a petty youthful offender. While I do not

condone the actions of the anonymous killer I will say that other officers should see this as a

reminder to not abuse your power." As Mayor Riker stepped down from the podium cameras

flashed and random people talked among themselves.

I turned off the television and sat down trying to remind myself that what I saw on

television minutes ago was in fact real. Ironically the mayor didn't criticize whoever he thought

had killed Michaels. I threw some clothes on and headed downstairs to the front desk to turn in

my key. Before leaving the hotel I grabbed a newspaper and headed to my car. Sure enough

Michaels death was pretty much the only thing that was mentioned in todays paper. It took up

so many pages in the paper I was surprised "The Funnies" section didn't lose its space for the day. I headed back to Hillsborough County I needed to make a visit to the station and have a

nice long chat with Hamilton. Even though I couldn't stand Linda I made it my business to get

information about her funeral arrangements.

I planned to do everything I could to make others believe I had nothing to do with her

death. As I got onto Fletcher Avenue from I-275 I headed west and noticed that there were at

least one or two police cruisers for every intersection. I viewed this as motivation to plan my

next kills carefully. I parked my car at a gas station and called Hamilton. "Captain how are things

at the station?" "Ace this is no time for bad questions, listen I can't say much over the phone

why don't you meet me for lunch somewhere on North Dale Mabry?" "Sounds good Captain I'll

see you at The Ale house.

Hamilton and I sat down at a booth and discussed my most recent kill. "Listen Ace I

Understand that your method of operation is to cool off for a little bit after you make a kill however since Linda's death could not be passed off as suicide you are going to have to pick up

the pace on the surviving members. So far you have not been named a suspect but in case you

haven't read the papers or watched the news the police around here are getting anxious and

ready to kill anyone that so much as looks them cross eyed. And it isn't just Linda's death that

has everyone worked up due to the mayor's comments yesterday he isn't exactly popular with

the force."

"Okay Captain here is what we are going to do, after we leave here we will go back

to the station call all of our deputies for a meeting and tell them to patrol various parts of the

Tampa area after Linda's funeral. We will keep the surviving members of Linda's group out of

this particular search because they were so close to her. With all of our deputies occupied this

makes my targets easier to hit." "Okay Ace, we will carry this one out as you have requested,

lets get back to the station." Hamilton and I returned to the station to share our plan on how we were going to find the one responsible for Linda's death, and discuss the time and place of

her funeral. Little did everyone know that the killer was right in their midst. It was empowering

to know that I had so much control over the department and that no one around me would

ever suspect that I was involved.

That was exactly the situation, no one currently working with me considered me a

suspect however Martinez who resigned from the force was certain that I was responsible for

Linda's death as well as Corso's even though he couldn't prove it. Two days later Linda's funeral

was held at the same cemetery as Reggaes. I kept my word and attended just so I could cover

my ass. I kept looking to see if Martinez would be there but he was nowhere in sight. However

Bradford, Jacobs, and Matthews were there to pay respect. After the funeral the three of them

approached me requested that I put them on the case. "Gentlemen I can't do that, you were

too close to Linda I have my orders."

I knew that I was going to have speed things up so later that evening I made a visit to the station so I could make note of the weekly schedule for my next three victims. I knew for a fact that these three weren't going to follow my orders that easily so I decided to make a hit on both Kyle and Gary on the same night. With the weekend almost over I waited until Tuesday night to make the hit. Tuesday was a drinking night for both Kyle and Gary and if my suspicions were correct they would be at a bar somewhere on Hillsborough Avenue. And since these two loved to abuse their power they would even go as far as drinking while wearing their police uniforms.

I found two police cruisers in the parking lot, I looked inside and sure enough they were both in there wearing their uniforms as if they were trying to intimidate those around them. I watched them for a few minutes and monitored their behavior, they clearly had too much to drink. Especially because they were harassing the waitress that was attending to them. I caught

them in the act putting their hands on her and laughing loudly at her embarrassment and

disapproval of their advances. I couldn't hear what was being said but I could see that other

guests were becoming quite irritated with Kyle and Gary's disrespectful actions. Moments later

a large man approached them and pointed toward the door. Apparently that man was the

general manager, and he was making it clear they had to leave. They got up form their seats

and proceeded to mock him before exiting.

They walked toward their cruisers in a rather clumsy manner, after entering their

vehicles they headed west on Hillsborough. They made a right hand turn onto Anderson Road

where I continued my pursuit. I saw them park their cruisers at a gas station on the right hand

side. I parked near them and waited for a few minutes. I noticed a homeless man sitting down

in front of the gas station. It was closed at the moment and I guess he saw no harm in his actions. Kyle and Gary felt different, they emerged from their cruisers and walked toward the

homeless man. In their drunken rage they lifted him up and took turns hitting him and shoving

him to the ground. They even kicked him while he was down.

I stepped out of my car and fired a few shots in the air. Although they were drunk they

were well aware of my presence. They stormed toward me and demanded that I leave the area.

I responded by reaching in my jacket and pulling out an ooze. I fired at Gary's shin bone and

worked my way up to his throat. I turned to aim at Kyle and tore into his kneecap. He fell to the

ground screaming in pain. I stood over him and demanded information about Martinez.

"What's Martinez up to? And don't you dare lie to me!" "Ace I really have no idea of his

whereabouts, please you have to get me to a hospital I won't tell anyone what you did."

"Wrong answer Kyle, this is going to be a long night." I went to my car and grabbed a bottle of bleach, I poured a good amount of it on Kyle's open wound.

Within a few seconds he told me what I needed to hear. "Ace, Martinez hasn't forgotten about you, in fact he has spoken with me and the others about how he has wanted to get back at you. I also want you to know that Harold Martin is now a part of his group. One more thing, Monday night on May 6, Martinez and Harold will be doing a weapons deal with a local gang, I'm not sure where but I think Bruce has the information involving its whereabouts." "You did the right thing Kyle, but unfortunately you don't deserve medical treatment." I fired at Kyle's head and watched the bullets tear through him splattering fragments of his skull and brain matter on the ground. I dragged Gary's corpse over to Kyle's and I drenched their dead bodies in bleach and set their remains on fire.

After leaving the scene I intended to do my usual routine after a kill, go home and sleep it off. Little did I know trouble would be waiting for me at my home. As I pulled into my driveway I noticed a large hole in my window. I slowly walked toward the door holding my revolver close to my chest. The lights were still off so I had to plan each move carefully as I opened the door I felt the barrel of a gun lightly press against my head. “Drop your weapon Ace, it’s the end of the line for you.” I slowly laid my gun on my sofa and immediately grabbed the would be killers wrist and aimed his gun away from both of us. I balled up my right fist and hit him hard right in his jaw. I sent him flying into a wall. I grabbed his gun and flipped on a light switch.

I had never seen this man before but since he knew my name I knew for certain that he was working with Martinez. He slowly picked himself up off the floor, before he had a chance to fight back I yanked him up by his shirt and pistol whipped him repeatedly with his own gun. I then shoved him into my bathroom and slammed his face onto the end of the sink. He fell to the floor favoring his busted nose. I pinned him to the floor with my knee in his chest then

reached under the sink and found a bottle of drain cleaner. I grabbed his throat forcing his

mouth open. As he fought for air I forcefully fed him the drain cleaner. I then stood over him

and watched as he convulsed and projected vomit and blood. Within a couple of minutes he

was dead. I searched his pockets and found his wallet along with a smart phone.

According to his drivers license his name was Ryan Philips. I decided to keep his

belongings and not inform other officers of his identification. I called for an ambulance and

ended up waiting for nearly an hour. When they arrived they had quite the story to tell me.

"Lieutenant McMillan sorry we are late is has been one hell of an evening." I assumed they

were talking about what had happened earlier that night so I decided to play dumb. "Hey guys

we all get busy what happened if you don't mind me asking?" "Well Lieutenant two more officers were killed tonight, whoever it is isn't resting anytime soon." "After what happened to

me in my house I get the feeling there is more than one killer."

As I saw the facial expressions of the paramedics I kept going with my thoughts on

tonight's events. "Let me ask the two of you a question who were the officers that were killed

earlier tonight?" "Lieutenant deputy Matthews and Bradford were both murdered earlier this

evening via gunshot wounds and then set on fire." "Gentleman I understand that they were two

of the six officers involved in the killing of a youthful offender just a few years ago correct?"

"Yes Lieutenant that is correct, we are no detectives but we get the feeling that whoever is

committing theses crimes intends to kill all the officers involved in that young boys death.

Are you implying that the killer is after you as well Lieutenant? You weren't one of the officers

involved in that boys death why would the killer have any problem with you?"

"I never said our mystery killer wanted to kill me, all I'm saying is that there is a possibility that more than one is involved. However, the person who tried to kill me tonight wasn't particular about which cop he killed. Listen Fellas I am not going to stay here tonight I am going to either stay with a friend or I will crash at a motel for the night." I fled the area and headed toward Roy Haynes park so I could clear my head and check Ryan's phone. Martinez had sent a few texts. "Where are you at and what's going on with Ace?" This is what he had said in his most recent text. Since he didn't know Ryan was dead I decided to use this to my advantage.

"Martinez, Ace got away we will have to meet up tonight what is the plan?" I waited for a response and within minutes he had this to say. "Ok well here's the plan, Jacobs is going to go into work tomorrow and resign from the force. This way he can cover his ass for when we take out Ace. Meet me at the dog track on Waters Avenue, Jacobs, Martin, and a few others will be with me." "Ok Martinez, text me a picture of your exact location so I can touch base with you

right away, I don't want to look suspicious." Martinez texted me a pic of the inside of the

stadium, along with a picture of the fifteen gang members he was conducting the weapons deal

with. I rushed toward the location and saw cop car after cop car on my way to the track.

With the current circumstances I knew this was going to be extremely dangerous but I

was so close to destiny at this point that nothing was going to stand in my way. I arrived at the

track at about one in the morning. I went inside and lurked around for a bit under the

bleachers. I peered through one of the breezeways and sure enough I saw Martinez, Jacobs,

and Martin facing the gang members. I watched them for a few minutes and took pictures of

them, this way if I had to answer for my killings I had evidence to justify my actions. As they

went through their collection of weapons I threw a grenade toward the group. The explosion killed five gang members and severely wounded three. I ran toward the exit but stopped before

standing directly in front of the next breezeway.

I quickly turned around and four gang members came running through the breezeway

behind me, I welcomed them by pulling out two oozes and firing at them. I ripped through all

four of them like a chainsaw. There were a total of six gang members alive at this point, three

of them couldn't move very fast due to the blast they survived from the grenade I had thrown

earlier. I tossed another grenade at the wounded members and watched their remains splatter

throughout the stadium. Martinez called Jacobs and Martin to his side. "WHAT THE HELL IS THIS

SHIT? WE NEED TO GET OUT OF HERE." Martinez and the other ex-deputies sprinted toward the

exit in fear for their lives.

The three surviving gang members were a little far behind them so I hid under the

bleachers and waited for them to run through the breezeway. As the third member barely entered the breezeway I took a knife and sliced through his jugular. His two friends turned

around and tried to attack me but it was too late I fired at both of them managed to hit them

directly between the eyes. I made my way toward the exit and saw Martinez scream frantically

in the parking lot before getting into his car. In the midst of his anxiety I fired two shots and hit

Jacobs in his chest, as he fell to the ground Martinez pulled out his phone and made a phone

call. That call happened to be for Ryan. "DAMMIT RYAN NEARLY EVERYONE IS DEAD WHERE

THE HELL ARE YOU?"

"Hey Martinez, five down two to go." For a moment or two there was silence on the

other line but I could still here Martinez breathing with anxiety. "Mark my words Ace you are

going to regret this, people are going to come looking for you." "Martinez tonight is your only

chance to kill me even if you win it will only make me a martyr." Martinez and Martin fled the

scene in separate vehicles I gave both of them a head start to make them think they would get away. I tracked Martins vehicle to an abandoned warehouse on a service road near Fowler Avenue. I knew Martin was inside the building so I slowly lurked around the area for a while.

I crept inside and all of the sudden the lights came on. “Hands in the air Lieutenant!” I put my hands up as I saw Martin aim a gun toward me. Instead of standing still I dove to my left behind an old forklift. Martin fired at me but ended up getting carried away which resulted in him running out of bullets. I didn’t get up right away just in case he had another gun. I looked in front of me and noticed a metal dolly used to wheel five gallon buckets of paint. I noticed the metal points at the end of the dolly and knew that it would hurt if those points were to pierce human flesh. I got up and saw Martin desperately trying to reload his gun. I forcefully pushed the dolly in his direction the dolly fell over backwards but continued to move forward. It went under his legs and stopped a few inches behind him with the metal points facing upward.

I aimed my gun and fired hitting him in his right shoulder. He fell down on top of the

dolly onto one of its sharp points. It penetrated the area just above the small of his back. He

screamed in agony and started coughing up blood. As much as I wanted him to suffer I had to

kill him quickly. I stood over him and stomped on his face and felt his skull crackle and pop

beneath my shoe. I jumped in my car and checked for Martinez's current location. Lucky for me

he wasn't far, he was at a water treatment facility located off of Nebraska Avenue located north

of the Fletcher Avenue intersection.

I arrived at the building rather quickly. I quietly entered the facility and Martinez leaped

from out of the shadows knocking me on the ground. I got up and roundhouse kicked him right

in his chest. He slowly rose to his feet and I responded by catching him in the chin with an

upper cut. I pinned him against the wall and reminded him of his actions that resulted in this

encounter. "Did you really think you were going to get away with Reggaes death?" Before he could respond I punched his face with a series of left and right hooks. He stood up against the wall bruised and bleeding I walked a few feet away from him making him think I was done with him. I turned around and ran toward him then I jump kicked him directly in his sternum.

He fell to the ground writhing in pain I forced him off the ground and drove rusty nails through both of his hands so he would stand up straight against the wall. I found a forklift and drove toward him. I pierced his stomach with one of the forklifts metal teeth mounting him against the wall. I stepped off the forklift and approached him. He was slowly dying, blood spewing out of his mouth and running down his chest. I reached in his pocket and found the keys to his cruiser. I had a feeling that he was carrying weapons in the trunk of his car. As I stepped away from Martinez I saw him close his eyes and stop moving.

Martinez along with his allies were finally slain and laid to rest. Although I had avenged

Reggaes death it didn't ease my pain nor was my mission over. Normally after a killing I would

go home and sleep, however at this point there was no going home, it all had to end before

the sun came up. I went through the trunk of Martinez's cruiser and found quite a bit of

weaponry, apparently I wasn't the only one who had gone shopping in the evidence locker.

I found a bazooka and more than enough rounds of ammunition. I also found an automatic

assault rifle and an m16. Within minutes I had loaded the material into the trunk of my Impala.

Before leaving the scene I placed a siren on top of my car and I made my way toward

Downtown Tampa. It was late but I wasn't tired I had to put a stop to the panel and make

extreme changes to the way law enforcement was run here in Florida. Hopefully my actions

would inspire the rest of our nation to adopt similar policies. Meanwhile District Attorney

Michael Reed was in his office located in Downtown Tampa with two older officers, I guess the panel was working odd hours. "Officers Will Thomas and Frank Carmen we have a problem

on our hands. Multiple Police Officers are being slaughtered one by one, a few more were killed

a few minutes ago. Mayor Roland Riker has painted this anonymous killer as a hero." "Reed

don't act so innocent, the police officers that have been killed committed crimes but were only

let off because they were cops."

"Will is right, on top of that they were still allowed to wear a badge because he

and I along with you and our last mayor pulled a few strings. Thanks to this unknown vigilante

more and more of our police officers are acting civil toward citizens." "Gentlemen you are

forgetting that even though this killer has wiped out bad people he took the law into his own

hands, he may come for us next." "Well Reed its only fair, Frank and I are ashamed for having

been apart of rehiring the officers that you grieve for." "Frank, Will what do the two of you

think you are doing?" "Will and I are doing what we should have done a long time ago, we are retiring. Here are our badges."

"DON'T WALK OUT OF HERE LIKE THIS IF YOU LEAVE NOW YOU'RE DEAD!" "To hell with

those two anyway, I have my own plans for taking out this vigilante, I can always hire more

protection." Upon making my way to the D.A's office building I saw both Will and Frank

exiting the building. I aimed the auto assault rifle at both of them and told them to go back into

the building and lead me to Reed's office. They obeyed without question and lead me to the

elevator. "So Lieutenant McMillan you are the one responsible for the killings?" "That's right

Frank, all of this was by my hands. Martinez had killed my supervisor Reggae Kenneth so before

I killed him I decided to go after his friends first that way he would have no choice but to face

me alone. Now I am here to take care of the panel so these mistakes are never made again."

"Ace I am sorry for your losses but as of tonight Frank and I are no longer members of the panel but we understand if you don't spare us, even though Reed and the former mayor

had pressured us we could have easily said no and retired then but we didn't so whatever you

do we understand." "Guys if you want to correct your mistakes just stick with me and tell me

everything I need to know before stepping into Reed's office." The elevator stopped on the

fifth floor as we stepped out both Will and Frank motioned me to not make too much noise

As we stood outside Reeds office I heard him on the phone having what sounded like a pretty

important conversation.

"Mayor Riker its me Reed listen you need to come here right away I know who the

vigilante is, be here in the next twenty minutes." Seeing as how the door of his office wasn't

fully closed I peered into the small opening and saw him standing up facing toward the window

looking down on the city softly talking to himself holding a gun. "As soon as Riker walks through

that door I will kill him and Frame Ace McMillan." I turned and looked at both Will and Frank and told them to do everything I told them to do. “Ok guys the second he walks away from that

window and sits down I need the two of you to knock on his door and tell him you forgot your

badges and that you want to be there so you can protect him from the vigilante.”

They both agreed with my plan and waited for a few minutes. Reed would soon take a

seat and my two friends would soon knock on his door. “Who is it?” “Reed its Will and Frank.”

“Come on in fellas what can I do for you?” As they entered his office I slowly stepped in the

room and saw Reed’s superior grin slowly fade and transform into a look of shock. Before he

could reach for his gun I fired two shots at him wounding him in his right arm and left leg. He

fell to the ground screaming in agony. “Tell me something Reed did I ruin your plans?”

“AAAAAAAHHHH WHAT ARE YOU TALKING ABOUT YOU ASSHOLE?” “Let me explain things to

you Reed, me and your former allies heard your plans about murdering Riker and Framing me.

I guess now I get my chance to finally meet the mayor." "Ok Ace you won just kill me and get

out of here."

"No Reed I'm not going to kill you, the mayor should be here any minute now and what

better way to ruin your life than to have you tell the mayor that you planned to kill him. Reed as

far as I'm concerned you are about to have a very bad day. Will and Frank you two can leave

anytime you want I can handle it from here." "No Ace, Frank and I are staying right here we

are in your corner." Around 3:30 that morning Mayor Riker had arrived, as soon as he saw me

Will, and Frank, standing next to Reed's wounded body he headed toward us with caution.

"Lieutenant McMillan what is going on here?"

"Mayor, District Attorney Michael Reed was planning to kill you so he could frame me

for your death." "Its true Mayor we were right by Ace's side when we overheard Reed's plan."

"Reed is this true?" "Yes Mayor please get me to a hospital I know when I've been beaten."

I saw the look of disgust in Roland's eyes he looked like he had lost a loved one as he shook his head at Reed. He then turned his attention to me and asked me a question that I'm sure he already knew the answer to.

"So Ace it was you all along wasn't it?" "Yes Riker all of this was by my hands." "Ace why did it have to be this way?" "Well Riker when cops break the law it's either a warning or administrative leave with pay. None of this would have happened had the officers I destroyed received the proper sentences in the first place. You see these dog tags around my neck? These belonged to Reggae Kenneth, he was my friend and mentor he was the one person who helped me love life and he was taken from me! He lost his life to one of those monsters who had the audacity to call himself a cop!" At that moment Riker closed his eyes and took a deep breath before approaching me, he put his hand on my shoulder and gave me his sympathy.

"Son I can't tell you how sorry I am for what's happened I want you to know that

You have my support every step of the way. I am willing to give you whatever you want just

name your price." "Well Riker before I begin I have no beef with you whatsoever but, I do have

a large list of demands, plus with my skill, track record, and artillery I possess you are in no

position to tell me no." It was at that moment Riker noticed the large bag I was carrying

containing various weapons from the evidence locker and from the trunk of Martinez's cruiser

during his failed weapons deal. "Ace as of right now no demand you make is too big or small

however Reed has to be hauled out of here." "That's fine with me Riker however, I want

Hamilton and Lawrence to be here with the paramedics to make the arrest."

Without question Riker called both Lawrence and Hamilton to appear on the scene with

the paramedics. The paramedics were the first to arrive at Reeds office, this worried me

because I was afraid they would blow my cover however Hamilton and Lawrence were not far behind and told the Paramedics to get lost. "Alright Ace it is real early in the morning and cops are all over Tampa trying to hunt down a vigilante who has been murdering bad cops and now we are called here to find that you shot the district attorney? Hamilton and I demand explanations." "Well Lawrence if you must know I committed those killings, from Corso to Martinez, along with Jesse and Katie." "Ace do you realize what you have done? The city is a warzone, I understand the cops you had killed were murderers themselves but you went over the line! Hand over your badge you are no longer a cop."

"LAWRENCE THAT IS ENOUGH"! Cried Riker. "In case you forgot Ace saved my life. Reed was plotting to kill me and frame Ace for the murder. Ace has both Will and Frank to vouch for him not to mention Reed was quick to confess what he was planning." "Riker is right Lawrence don't throw everything at Ace. Even though I had no involvement in his murders I did help supply him with some of his weapons and I did encourage him to commit the killings of those officers." "Lawrence before you say anything else let me remind you that the officers t Ace

murdered should have been booted off the force along time ago. However even as Chief Of

Police I realize you only have so much power. Before we go home Ace has a list of demands that

he would like to make, and due to his heroic acts I will do everything in my power to make

these demands a reality.

"First and foremost there will be equal treatment among citizens and police officers

when a crime is committed. Also, when an officer is killed in the line of duty it will be treated

the same as if a citizen had been killed. Now in case Mayor Riker hasn't mentioned anything to

Lawrence and Hamilton I am in no position to obey!" "Ace don't worry Hamilton and I heard

your message loud and clear and we will honor your demands, however we do ask that you

hand over your weapons. Another thing Ace Hamilton and I want to see you in my office later

today."

"Lawrence, Hamilton I hope you make room for me I will be there as well." As we left

Reeds office and went home I took the time to think about all the things I had done, I was

proud to know that I had made a difference I just hoped that this was going to pay off in the

long run. I didn't feel too safe sleeping at my home due to what had happened a few hours ago

so I decided to get a hotel for the evening. I was so anxious about my meeting that I barely

slept. As day broke I jumped out of bed grabbed some food and sped toward Lawrence's office.

Here I am back where I started earlier in my story wondering what my future held for me. As I

stepped into Chief Lawrence's office everyone who said they would attend kept their word.

Riker was there just as he had promised.

Believe it or not the governor of Florida himself Scott Richards was here to attend this

get together. He wasn't the only surprise guest however next to him were two well dressed men carrying folders. Lawrence sat down and motioned for me to take a seat. He then showed

me a newspaper depicting the murders committed by me however my name was not

mentioned in the paper. In fact the only people who truly knew that I was the killer were the

people attending the meeting with me along with Will and Frank who I had met just the other

night.

"Ace in case you haven't already figured it out your killings have attracted quite a bit of

Attention, you have practically brought the city of Tampa to its knees. Tell me Ace, do you think

your killings were justified?" "Yes Chief as a matter of fact I do, and seeing as I'm an officer of

the law the worst you can do to me is tell me is fire me or give me a letter of resignation."

After making my smart assed comments I sat back and proceeded to lean back in my chair and

rest my feet on Lawrence's desk. Despite the awkward silence throughout the room and the

look of disapproval on the chief's face I maintained my big smile. "Ok both of you knock it off, were here to talk business not fight! Let us not forget that even though the actions of Ace

McMillan were extreme he not only saved my life but he exposed corruption in his force and he

is also the reason why certain changes are going to be made within the Florida Department Of

Law Enforcement. Chief Lawrence if you will please let Governor Richards sit at your desk he

needs to go over a few things with Lieutenant McMillan."

As Governor Richards sat down he reached out and gave me a good firm handshake.

"Ace it is nice to meet you however I am going to have to make this short and sweet, Riker

informed me of your demands and believe me these policies will go into effect however that

means that any cop with a bad work record, is a threat to colleagues or citizens will

face termination. With that said there is a possibility that some of those officers will retaliate

but as you already know no one but the people in this room know who the real killer is."

"Richards even if they knew I was the killer it's just another day at the office for me."

"Ace you are arrogant but you know how to get the job done." Laughed Richards, "Ace it has

been a pleasure chatting with you but I have other matters to tend to."

Richards shook my hand and headed toward the door. At that moment the two suits

standing up against the wall approached the chiefs desk. I was beginning to feel sorry for

Lawrence he looked as if he really wanted to just have a seat at his desk in peace. As the two

men sat down at Lawrence's desk I had a bad feeling about them. I thought to myself "What if

these two guys are lawyers for the people I had killed?" That's when I decided to try and

intimidate them a little. "Look guys the only people that dress as nice as you are either lawyers

or FBI agents, I'm guessing the two of you are lawyers?"

They looked at one another and laughed. "Lieutenant McMillan we are neither just sit

back and relax. My name is Agent Torres and this is Agent Philips we represent a private organization that specializes in immediate sentencing of criminals." "Agent Torres and I have

heard a lot about you and your reputation, we were quite impressed with your tactics. You are

exactly what our organization is looking for you possess great strength and fighting ability but

you are also proficient with firearms." "Agent Philips and I would love to have you on our team,

you would have more authority than you have now and you would have a much bigger salary.

You would also get to travel throughout nation after all you of all people could really use a

vacation."

Lawrence looked over at me with pleading eyes either he wanted me to take the

promotion or he just wanted to sit down at his desk. I knew that I was going to accept the offer

however I wanted to screw with Lawrence one last time. "I don't know fellas your offer sounds

tempting but how do I know this is genuine?" That's when Lawrence finally broke down. "OH

FOR THE LOVE OF GOD JUST TAKE THE GOD DAMN PROMOTION GUYS CAN'T YOU SEE HE IS

ONLY DOING THIS TO SCREW WITH ME?" Torres and Philips nearly fell over laughing after

witnessing Lawrence's tantrum. "Take it easy there Chief I am more than happy to take their

offer besides you need a little bit of weight off of your shoulders.

"Ok fellas all kidding aside when do I start working for you?" "Well Ace why don't you

take about three months off and get back to Philips and myself. Until then why don't you take

this check as our way of saying welcome aboard." My eyes grew to the size of golf balls when I

saw the size of that check, "Five-hundred thousand. "Agent Torres and Agent Philips big thank

you to the both of you." "Ace it was nice meeting you but Torres and I have to run, see you in

three months." I walked toward the door but before I could leave Lawrence called me back to

his office. "Ace before you go it was a pleasure having you on my force even though you drove me up the wall from time to time you were a great cop it won't be the same without you, be

careful out there." I smiled and waved goodbye. Upon leaving the force my demands were met

Mayor Riker and Governor Richards were more than happy to honor me. On top of that they

kept my identity secret.

District Attorney Reed was stripped of his position and sentenced to life in prison. He

will receive no special treatment. Captain Hamilton decided to take a little vacation outside of

Florida for a bit. He calls me from time to time to keep me posted about how things are at the

station. As for me I am going to make the most of my vacation, however that doesn't mean that

I am going to ignore criminal activity. Remember, whether you are a citizen or an authority

figure I will be watching you.

THE END

Written by Terry Dante

Special thanks to my loved ones both friends and family. Especially to you Uncle Merrell

McMillan, Ace's last name is a nod to you.

Also special thanks and appreciation to the original artist

of the piece that I have used as my cover.

Made in the USA
Monee, IL
04 November 2026

67352883R00066